GREAT DISASTERS

THE SAN FRANCISCO EARTHQUAKE

JOHN DUDMAN

Illustrated by Richard Scollins

The Bookwright Press
New York · 1988

Great Disasters

The Destruction of Pompeii
The San Francisco Earthquake
The Space Shuttle Disaster
The Sinking of the Titanic

First published in the
United States in 1988 by
The Bookwright Press
387 Park Avenue South
New York, NY 10016

First published in 1988 by
Wayland (Publishers) Limited
61 Western Road, Hove
East Sussex BN3 1JD, England

ISBN 0-531-18163-4
Library of Congress Catalog Card Number: 87-73160

Typeset by Oliver Dawkins, Burgess Hill, West Sussex, England.
Printed in Italy by G. Canale & C.S.p.A, Turin

Cover ***Refugees look out over the remains of San Francisco.***

Words that are printed **bold** the first time they appear in the text are explained in the glossary.

CONTENTS

A SHAKING CITY

Police Sergeant Jesse Cook was standing on a street corner in San Francisco at 5:12 a.m. on April 18, 1906 when he saw the earthquake approaching. The road rose and fell in great ripples. "It was as if the waves of the ocean were coming toward me . . ."

From under the ground a deep rumble grew into a deafening roar. Suddenly, Sergeant Cook was sent reeling as towering office blocks swayed, **masonry** crashed to the ground and windows shattered.

In hotels and homes across the city, people were thrown from their beds. Buildings and bridges collapsed, cable car tracks twisted like strips of licorice, water and gas mains burst and fires spread through the city.

The two-minute earthquake, and the inferno that raged for three days afterward, left San Francisco devastated. The exact death toll is not known, but it was at least 500, and another 250,000 were left homeless. Three thousand acres of offices, shops and houses in the heart of the city were flattened and charred. The damage was assessed at 500 million dollars — an amount that would be in the billions today.

San Francisco's ordeal was minor compared with other earthquakes. But it

has been the most researched of all the world's natural disasters because the city lies across the San Andreas Fault, a crack in the earth's crust, thirty-two kilometers (20 mi) deep, that runs the length of California under one of the most highly populated areas in the United States.

The tensions radiating from the grinding underground rock faces beneath the North American continent and the Pacific Ocean seabed have been constantly monitored by scientists since the earthquake of 1906.

"Will it happen again?" is the question they are trying to answer. Their reply is a firm "yes." But they cannot predict the time of the next big earthquake, when the death toll and damage will be much greater than it was in 1906.

Above *California Street Hill before the earthquake of 1906.*

Below *Sergeant Cook was hurled to the ground by the earthquake.*

THE GOLDEN CITY

San Francisco had been the capital of the American West since the historic gold rush of 1849. It was a rich, thriving city in the spring of 1906.

San Francisco crowns a range of hills on a **peninsula** forty-eight kilometers (30 mi) long making up the lower lip of a beautiful bay with an entrance known as the Golden Gate.

Below *This map shows the city's position on the California coast.*

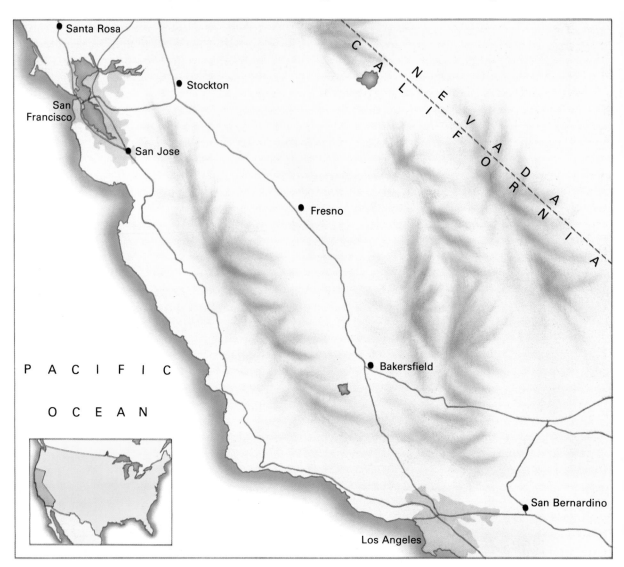

Above ***Chinatown market in San Francisco before the 1906 earthquake.***

An Englishman called William Richardson launched San Francisco's commercial life when he settled there in 1835. He began by collecting hides of wild animals using their fat to make candles. He bought two **schooners** to trade with San José, a settlement about sixty kilometers (37 mi) to the south. Richardson prospered and became the acknowledged captain of the port of San Francisco.

The population grew steadily from a few thousand to more than 400,000 by 1906. By then, San Francisco was a **cosmopolitan** city ruled by wealthy businessmen. They had arrived seeking fortune after the opening of the Central Pacific railroad followed the discovery of gold. Success produced wealth for the mine owners, railroad millionaires and commercial leaders, who established themselves in luxurious homes on Nob Hill that overlooked the financial heart of the city.

Many nationalities lived in San Francisco creating a multi-cultural community. The waterfront, known as the Barbary Coast, thrived with sailors from the Americas, Russia and the **Orient** who drank, danced and often fought in the dance halls and bars. Thousands had settled there including South Sea Islanders, Europeans, North American Indians and Chinese.

An unsuspecting city

Above ***Part of the luxurious Palace Hotel, which was destroyed in 1906.***

There had been earthquakes in 1856, 1872 and 1898, and although buildings were damaged, the warning shocks failed to alert the population to the fearful power that lay beneath its feet. Indeed, by the turn of the century, optimism had replaced any feeling of apprehension. Even so, new buildings were strengthened to withstand any future tremors. The six-million-dollar City Hall, the new post office, hotels and business blocks had been built symbolizing confidence and wealth.

In 1906, nobody was prepared for the earthquake that was to cause so much destruction and chaos. The devastation left thousands of people without homes, and millions of dollars were needed to rebuild San Francisco.

Below *The City Hall, one of the many important buildings that collapsed during the earthquake.*

Beneath the Pacific Ocean

Out at sea about 240 kilometers (150 mi) west of San Francisco, the bow of the schooner *John A. Campbell* rose suddenly and crashed back onto the sea. A frightened crew leaped from their bunks, fearing a collision. But when they reached the deck, the sea was quite calm. Closer to the coast, a steamer keeled over as an invisible punch buckled its sides.

The earthquake hit the coast 145 kilometers (90 mi) north of San Francisco. A lighthouse, thirty meters (98 ft) high, swayed so violently that its beacon exploded. Forests of giant beechwood trees were demolished and hundreds of miles away other trees bowed to the

Below ***Out on the Pacific Ocean, the terrified crew of a schooner were hit by the invisible force.***

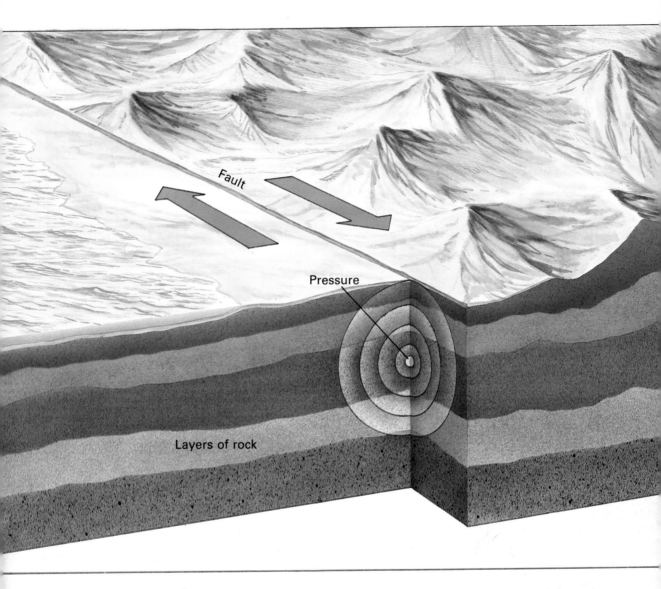

Labels on image: Fault, Pressure, Layers of rock

Above *Pressure can reach such a level that layers of rock snap and cause an earthquake.*

unseen force. Cliffs slid into the sea, trains were suddenly tossed sideways, buildings crumbled in villages and towns, as the earth disintegrated deep underneath the ground.

In San Francisco's central market, horses panicked, suddenly neighing and rearing. In the city zoo, lions roared and other animals scampered around their pens in fright. "There was a deep and terrible rumble," Sergeant Cook recalled. "Then I could see it actually coming up Washington Street. The whole street was rippling."

A shattered population

The first shock lasted for forty seconds. A few moments of astonished silence was broken by chiming church bells and the cries of the injured. There then followed two more tremors that violently shook the city. House after house collapsed as the shock waves swept across San Francisco. Overhead electric power lines snapped in showers of blue sparks.

In the editorial office of the *San Francisco Examiner,* news editor John Barrett had also heard the approaching earthquake. He and his colleagues were sent staggering. From their windows they saw office blocks tottering. "It was as though the earth was slipping away under our feet. There was a sickening sway and we were knocked flat on our faces."

In the Palace Hotel, Arthur Gould from

Chicago, was thrown from his bed half way across the room. Grabbing his clothes, he ran in his pyjamas down six flights of stairs into the lobby. "The clerks and hotel employees were running about as if they were mad. Other guests appeared. Few wore more than their night clothes."

Guests, awakened by the tremors, fill the Palace Hotel's lobby.

Gould walked in his bare feet to the nearby Western Union office to send a telegram to his wife in Los Angeles only to discover that all the lines were down. "I sat on the sidewalk, picked the broken glass out of my feet and put on my clothes." Around him, fire had engulfed three office blocks.

Enrico Caruso, an internationally famous Italian opera singer of the period, was in San Francisco with The Metropolitan Opera company at the time of the earthquake. Alfred Hertz, the company''s conductor, ran from his wrecked bedroom to Caruso's suite. He found the famous tenor in hysterics. Furniture, carpets and clothes had been scattered around the room. Caruso whispered that he feared he had lost his voice.

Hertz led him to the open window. They looked out on crowds of frightened people, some half-naked, running down the street with belongings clasped in their arms. Hertz tapped the sill and ordered Caruso to sing. The tenor sang with the full power of his voice, bringing the survivors in the street to a standstill to gaze in awe at the man high above them. A few minutes later Caruso, dressed splendidly in striped trousers and jacket was escorted from the shattered hotel to make his escape out of San Francisco with the other **refugees**.

By then a black cloud of smoke hung over the stricken city. The fires from broken gas mains were spreading with alarming speed.

CATASTROPHE

From his home on Nob Hill, Brigadier General Frederick Funston, deputy commander of a U.S. Army post, had watched San Francisco collapse street by street. When he saw fire after fire break out amid the devastation he acted without hesitation.

He ordered his troops into the burning streets to fight the flames, rescue the injured and shoot **looters** on sight. He called in reinforcements and gave his forces complete control. Only then did Funston give orders to notify Washington of his plans and afterward informed Mayor Eugene Schmitz that San Francisco was under military rule.

Below *The extent of the damage to San Francisco was devastating.*

Left **Police give flour rations to the refugees of the San Francisco earthquake.**

Below **Homeless refugees were forced to live in shacks.**

The mayor had already taken action himself. He had called a meeting of fifty prominent citizens. A relief committee was formed to organize refugee camps and canteens to feed the homeless. A night **curfew** was imposed.

As they considered the desperate situation, the City Hall, hotels, theaters, banks, offices and waterfront **wharfs**, were all being engulfed by fire. The mayor and his advisers ran from one make-shift office to another as the fires approached. Slowly they managed to co-ordinate the police and one thousand firemen into a well-organized rescue operation.

In a suburb across town, a housewife started what became known as "The Ham and Eggs Fire." After the earthquake subsided, she decided to cook some breakfast. Without knowing that her chimney had collapsed, she lit her stove and within seconds, her home was alight. A breeze blew the flames on to neighboring houses and turned the entire block into an inferno.

15

Amid the wreckage

In those first appalling hours as the fires took hold, Mayor Schmitz's committee confirmed that all looters would be shot on sight. Stores were being raided and **corpses** plundered. There were incidents involving survivors, who had turned on looters and murdered them in the charred frameworks of burned buildings. A soldier who saw a thief trying to bite an earring off a dead woman's ear shot him immediately. Even a baker who demanded high prices for his bread was reported to have been executed because the mayor had issued an order against **profiteering**. There were also actions of extreme courage and mercy — survivors trapped beneath rubble, as fire moved toward them,

pleaded with soldiers to be shot. Seeing no alternative, the soldiers granted their desperate wishes.

Right **This sign shows the chaos suffered during the earthquake.**

Below **Amid the wreckage, soldiers were ordered to shoot anyone stealing from ruins and corpses.**

Blasting the fires

Above ***Soldiers blew up a street in an attempt to block off the fires.***

It was the destructive fires, raging for three days, that caused more havoc and damage than the earthquake itself. The first shock awakened Fire Chief Dan Sullivan who, jumping from his bed, fell to his death through a hole in the floor. Yet his fire-fighting force needed no orders to take action.

They ran to their stations, manned the engines and drove into the shattered streets to the nearest **hydrants**. They connected their hoses and waited for the water to burst out. But only a thin trickle emerged — the three main water pipes had been severed.

Left *The fires that raged after the earthquake almost ruined the city of San Francisco.*

Below *In the city streets, firemen failed to subdue the flames with fire engines.*

So they sought supplies from reservoirs, pools, sewers and even the ocean, but their efforts could not hold back the wall of flames.

Without water supplies, the firemen collected dynamite and gunpowder to blast through the city an avenue one and a half kilometers (1 mi) long and 150 meters (492 ft) wide to stop the flames from spreading any farther. A series of explosions brought down tottering ruins, halting the flames temporarily. Troops moved in with **artillery** to level other burning buildings in the hope of putting out the fires.

The U.S. Mint survives

Amid the flames, smoke and heat, one building managed to hold out against the onslaught. The granite and sandstone United States **Mint**, which stored twenty million dollars in coins and **bullion** in its vaults, was defended by fifty employees using their own water supply — a system installed only ten days before. Sheets of flames sixty meters (197 ft) high ate up office blocks as they roared toward the mint. Soldiers and firemen soaked the building floor by floor with water from its own underground well.

Howard French, an employee at the mint, recalls, "The fire leapt up Mint Avenue in solid masses of flame . . . blinding and suffocating smoke forced us to abandon the hoses, and the fighters

Below *Makeshift tents and huts were built to house refugees left homeless after the disaster.*

retreated . . . down in the depths where untold wealth was so well safeguarded, artillerymen protected by blankets, coughed in the stifling smoke. There was a lull in the fire and so the fire-fighters returned to the upper stories. The roof was swept by a hose, cooling the copper surface until it became safe to walk on.''

An army officer, axe in hand, tore up sections of the blazing roof, beneath which a stream of water was directed. At 4 p.m. the United States Mint was announced out of danger, leaving a charred and glassless front.

Throughout the next day, the fires burned almost unchecked, sweeping through Nob Hill and other high-class residential areas. Columns of smoke rose hundreds of feet into the sky, signaling to surrounding towns the destruction of the great port.

Toward the end of the week, supplies of food, clothing, tents and medicine were arriving from all over the United States while the fires still raged. Churches were turned into hospitals; temporary altars were put up in open spaces for services and even weddings, as engaged couples decided to wait no longer. In the panic, about 70,000 people had escaped in ferry boats to the town of Oakland across the bay. But many survivors stayed behind to look for missing friends and relatives in the smoking streets, gradually making their way to refugee camps on higher ground.

An eyewitness account

From one of the hills, an eyewitness described the scene as the heart of the city burned.

"A sea of liquid fire lay beneath us. The sky above seemed to burn at white heat, deepening into gold and orange and spreading into a fierce glare. The smoke had gathered into one gigantic cloud that hung, motionless . . . the fire engulfed a church here, a block of houses there, and a steeple flaring high like a torch toppled and fell in a shower of sparks."

The fires had burned themselves out by Saturday; the next day the air was clear. There had been 490 city blocks destroyed in an area six times the size of that swept by the Great Fire of London in 1666. Then the rain fell in torrents. A week later the street cars were running, electricity supplies were functioning and the telephone system was working again.

Below *The sky was filled with smoke as the city burned.*

Left *When the fires subsided the extent of the damage could be seen. It was a tragic sight for San Franciscans.*

RUBBLE TO RICHES

Six years after the earthquake the scars were hidden by 20,000 new buildings. San Francisco had recovered from its terrifying ordeal and was inviting the world to see the evidence of its courageous recovery by staging an international exhibition.

Indeed, the city became very much a part of the growing wealth of California, which was marked particularly in the 1930s by Hollywood film studios. After World War II, industry expanded even more with the establishment of oil and engineering corporations along with the development of science and new technology.

Yet San Francisco and other towns remain realistic about the hidden threat from the San Andreas Fault. For this huge crack in the earth represents the division between the great plates beneath the

Below *A 1920s view of the new financial area.*

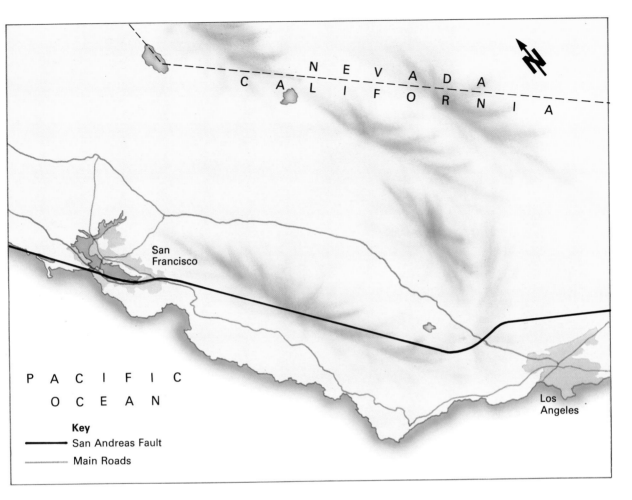

Key
— San Andreas Fault
--- Main Roads

North Pacific Ocean and North America. These enormous slabs of the world's crust are constantly grinding against each other, causing tremors that normally produce little damage.

The **earth's plates**, under the continents and oceans, are always on the move. Below the Atlantic Ocean they are drifting apart, separating Europe and North America at a rate of about four centimeters (1.6 in) a year. In South America, the plates are pressing against each other, and the Pacific Ocean floor is

Above ***The San Andreas Fault, which caused the 1906 earthquake.***

sliding slowly beneath the continent.

On either side of the San Andreas Fault the plates move beside each other. The Pacific plate moves northwest at an annual rate of five centimeters (2 in). Los Angeles, which rests on this plate west of the Fault, approaches San Francisco by about a quarter of a meter (10 in) every six years. During the earthquake of 1906 it moved three meters (10 ft) nearer.

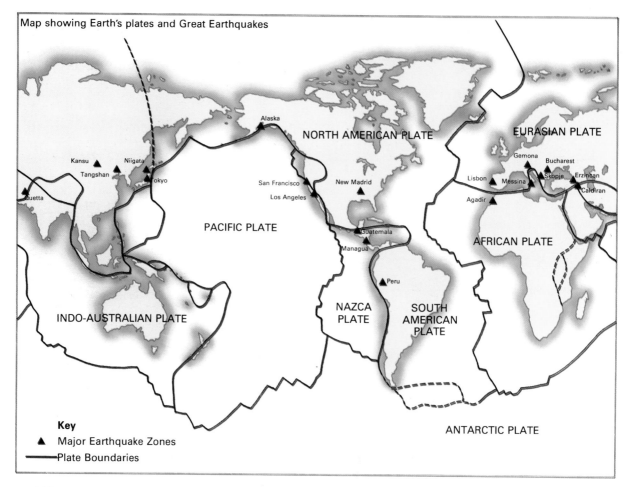

Map showing Earth's plates and Great Earthquakes

NORTH AMERICAN PLATE

EURASIAN PLATE

Kansu

Niigata

Tangshan

Tokyo

Quetta

Alaska

San Francisco

New Madrid

Los Angeles

Gemona

Bucharest

Lisbon

Skopje

Erzincan

Messina

Caldiran

Agadir

PACIFIC PLATE

AFRICAN PLATE

Guatemala

Managua

Peru

INDO-AUSTRALIAN PLATE

NAZCA
PLATE

SOUTH
AMERICAN
PLATE

Key

▲ Major Earthquake Zones

—— Plate Boundaries

ANTARCTIC PLATE

Will it happen again?

Seismologists, who have been studying the San Andreas Fault for many years, fear that San Francisco is due for another devastating earthquake. They believe that a jolt matching the 1906 shock could result in a death toll of 23,000 and cause the destruction of billions of dollars worth of property.

Between 1959 and 1975, seismologists discovered that an area of 51,500 square kilometers (19,884 sq mi) north of Los

Above *This map shows the earth's plates and earthquake zones.*

Angeles, had risen by nearly half a meter (1½ ft). However, it then began to subside.

From 1972 to 1979, the land east of Los Angeles came under subterranean pressure. Around San Francisco, the San Andreas Fault has remained stationary for many decades, although tremendous pressure has been building up on all sides and has occasionally been released in comparatively minor tremors.

These earth tremors rate only low readings on the **Richter scale** that measures the power and extent of earthquakes. These measurements were devised by Dr. Charles Richter, a leading seismologist, on an open-ended scale, which assesses the energy of an earthquake and thus its strength.

The extent of the damage is determined by how close to the surface an earthquake occurs, and whether or not it is near a highly populated area.

Below *The dotted line shows the position of the San Andreas Fault in San Francisco.*

Recent quakes

While fire was the greatest hazard produced by the San Francisco earthquake of 1906, today there are additional dangers. The mountain dams and artificial lakes above cities such as Los Angeles could send floods into the ruins of an earthquake-stricken city with devastating results.

Scientists are agreed that one day the earth beneath California will move and produce "the big one." There have been warnings in recent years.

On August 18, 1982 a minor tremor made buildings move slightly in San Francisco. There was little damage, and nobody was killed or injured.

On April 24, 1984 another tremor caused skyscrapers to sway in the city. In offices people saw plate glass windows bending as buildings moved on their foundations. The tremor, which lasted twenty seconds, spread over 320 kilometers (199 mi), damaging houses in a farming town and injuring twenty-one people, five of them children.

On April 1, 1986 another rolling earthquake caused skyscrapers to move again. Power lines snapped and crockery was sent flying in many homes. Five people were slightly injured. As in 1906, the threat remains constant for the residents of San Francisco.

Below *Today San Francisco lives in constant fear of "the big one."*

GLOSSARY

Artillery   Cannons or any mounted guns bigger than a machine gun.
Bullion   Brick-shaped blocks of gold or silver.
Corpses   Dead bodies, especially those of human beings.
Cosmopolitan   Inhabited by people from many different countries.
Curfew   An official order to the people of a city to stay in their houses and not to go out for a period of time.
Earth's plates   The layers of rock that make up the hard outer layer of the earth's crust.
Hydrant   An upright pipe with a valve attached from which water can be released to fight fires. Hydrants are located on town and city streets
Looters   People who steal goods at a time of war, rioting or turmoil.
Masonry   The stones and bricks used to construct buildings.
Mint   A place where money is made.
Orient   The countries that make up the eastern part of the world.
Peninsula   A narrow piece of land that juts out into the sea from the mainland.
Profiteering   Charging very high prices for goods that are in short supply.
Refugees   People who have had to leave their homes because of danger, and are left homeless.
Richter scale   A scale that measures the strength of an earthquake; it was introduced in 1935 by Charles Richter.
Schooners   Sailing boats with at least two masts and fore-and-aft sails.
Seismologists   Scientists who specialize in the study of earthquakes.
Wharfs   Wooden, stone or concrete platforms at the edge of a harbor for boats to load and unload their goods.

FURTHER READING

Disastrous Hurricanes and Tornadoes by Max and Charlotte Alth. Franklin Watts, 1981.
Earthquakes by Helen Challard. Children's Press, 1982.
Earthquakes: Nature in Motion by Hershell and Joan Nixon. Dodd, 1981.
Earthquakes and Volcanoes by Imelda and Robert Updegraff. Children's Book Company, 1981.

Earthquakes and Volcanoes by Laurence Santrey. Troll Associates, 1985.
Geological Disasters: Earthquakes and Volcanoes by Thomas G. Aylesworth. Franklin Watts, 1979.
How Did We Find Out About Earthquakes? by Isaac Asimov. Avon, 1981.
The Story of the San Francisco Earthquake by R. C. Stein. Children's Press, 1983.
Why Do We Have Earthquakes? by Norita D. Larson. Creative Education, 1982.

EARTHQUAKES AROUND THE WORLD

Date	Place	Deaths
1755	Lisbon, Portugal	6,000
1866	Peru and Ecuador	25,000
1906	San Francisco, United States	700
1908	Messina, Italy	160,000
1920	Kansu, China	180,000
1923	Tokyo, Japan	143,000
1935	Quetta, Pakistan	60,000
1939	Erzincan, Turkey	40,000
1960	Agadir, Morocco	12,000
1963	Skopje, Yugoslavia	1,000
1964	Niigata, Japan	250
1964	Anchorage, Alaska, United States	100
1971	Los Angeles, United States	50
1972	Nicaragua	12,000
1975	Bucharest, Rumania	1,500
1976	Guatemala	23,000
1976	Gemona, Italy	1,000
1976	Caldiran, Turkey	8,000
1976	Tangshan, China	500,000
1983	Eurzurum, Turkey	2,000
1985	Mexico City, Mexico	20,000

INDEX

ACKNOWLEDGMENTS

The illustrations on pages 6, 11, 25 and 26 are by Peter Bull.

The publishers would like to thank the following for providing the photographs in this book: BBC Hulton COVER, 15(t), 17(t), 19(r), 28; Photo Research International 14; Popperfoto 7, 8, 9, 19(l), 23(t), 24, 27; Topham Photo Library 15(b), 20, 21, 29.